Bad mit Aussicht. Die Wanne in einer Suite des Silo Hotels gewährt einen Blick über die V&A Waterfront Richtung Signal Hill. Der Gebäudekomplex, früher als Getreidesilo genutzt, befindet sich direkt neben dem Zeitz Museum of Contemporary Art Africa (MOCAA). ::: Bathroom with a view. The tub of a suite in The Silo Hotel looks out over V&A Waterfront towards Signal Hill. Once a working grain silo, now alongside the Zeitz Museum of Contemporary Art Africa (MOCAA).

Spätnachmittags hält eine Yacht aus Kap-eigener Produktion auf den Hafen zu. Tages- und Sundownertouren sind Teil einer lebhaften Segeltradition. Die dramatische Küstenlinie und die schwierigen Gewässer machen Kapstadt auch zu einer beliebten und wichtigen Zwischenetappe für internationale Segelrennen. ::: Late afternoon and a Cape-built yacht heads on towards the harbour. Cape Town's dramatic coastline and challenging waters make for a vibrant sailing tradition. Day sailing and sunset cruises are all part of the mix, but the city is also a popular and important staging point on the international racing circuit.

Alain Proust   Thomas Ernst   Peter Borchert

Delius Klasing Verlag

Der Tafelberg, schattenhaft im Nachglühen des Sonnenuntergangs, ragt wie eine Insel aus dem Ozean. Diese an ruhigen Tagen einladende Szenerie hat seit Jahrhunderten unzähligen Seglern das Ende einer langen Reise angezeigt. ::: Table Mountain, silhouetted against the afterglow of sunset, looms island-like from the ocean. On a calm day, this welcoming scene has marked the end of a long voyage for countless sailors across the centuries.

Verhangener Himmel über Weinbergen, die sich sanft hinunter bis zur Kellerei des Steenberg Estate ziehen, nur 30 Minuten Fahrt von Kapstadts Stadtzentrum entfernt. Die Anlage auf der ältesten Farm des Constantia-Tals, einer der besten Weingegenden am Kap, umfasst auch ein Fünfsternehotel und einen Golfplatz. ::: Cloudy skies over vineyards sweeping down to the wine cellar of Steenberg Estate, only a 30-minute drive from Cape Town's city centre. The Steenberg complex which includes a 5-star hotel and golf course sprawls across the oldest farm in the Constantia Valley, one of the Cape's finest wine-growing areas.

An lauen Sommerabenden besuchen Einheimische wie auch Touristen dienstags gern den Gemeindemarkt der Cape Point Vineyards in Noordhoek. Die lässige Kombination von Streetfood, Wein, Livemusik und herrlichen Ausblicken ist schwer zu toppen. In den Wintermonaten versammelt man sich gern drinnen am offenen Feuer. ::: On balmy summer evenings, locals and visitors alike head for the Thursday community market at the Cape Point Vineyards in Noordhoek. The casual combination of street-style food, wine, live music and beautiful vistas is hard to beat. In the colder winter months, the action moves around the open firepit inside.

Inhalt

Einleitung ::: Introduction   **12**

    Vergangenheit & Zukunft ::: Past & Future   16

Landschaft ::: Landscape   **18**

    Hochebene & Tiefebene ::: High plain & Lowlands   20

    Stadt & Land ::: Town & Rural   30

    Land & Meer ::: Land & Sea   36

    Atlantik & Indischer Ozean ::: Atlantic & Indian Ocean   54

    Festland & Inseln ::: Mainland & Islands   70

    Natur & Kulturlandschaft ::: Nature & Cultural Landscape   74

Gesellschaft ::: Society 84

Schwarz & Weiß ::: Black & White 86

Arm & Reich ::: Poor & Rich 92

Kulture ::: Culture 100

Streetfood & Gastronomie ::: Streetfood & Gastronomy 102

Bildende Kunst & Street-Art ::: Fine Art & Street Art 112

Entspannung & Sport ::: Relaxation & Sport 116

Moderne Architektur & Klassische Bauten :::
Modern Architecture & Vintage Buildings 130

Die Autoren ::: The Authors 150
Danksagung ::: Authors Acknowledgements 151
Karte und Adressen ::: Map and Addresses 152

Einleitung ::: Introduction

Sonnenuntergang-Fans wandern auf einem einstündigen Pfad den Lion's Head hinauf. Der Weg verlangt nicht schwindelfreien Menschen zwar ihren gesamten Mut ab, aber er ist die Anstrengung wert, besonders bei Vollmond, wenn die Lichter der Stadt bis in weite Ferne glitzern. ::: Sunset hikers on the hour-long trail that winds to the top of Lion's Head. It can be a scary haul for those without a head for heights, but well worth the effort, especially on a full moon evening with the city below twinkling into the distance.

Vergangenheit & Zukunft ::: Past & Future

Wann genau die ersten Menschen auf den Hängen des Tafelbergs standen und bestaunten, wie das Wasser aus der großen Bucht nach Norden brandete verliert sich in den Tiefen der Zeit. Die „älteste Zeichnung der Welt", ein Linienmuster, das mit einem Ocker-Stück gezeichnet wurde, ist etwa 73.000 Jahre alt und findet sich in einer Höhle 300 Kilometer östlich von Kapstadt. Hinweise legen nahe, dass die Phönizier diese Gegend vor 2.700 Jahren in ihren Gaulos-Seglern erreichten.

Abgesehen von diesen historischen Verbindungen ist Kapstadt mit einem Alter von weniger als 400 Jahren eine junge Stadt, verglichen mit den jahrtausendealten Hauptstädten und Siedlungen in Nordafrika. Aber sie ist die älteste Südafrikas, und ihre Geschichte ist tief verwurzelt mit dem Land und dessen Bewohnern.

Auf der Suche nach einem Seeweg zu den gewürzreichen Ufern Asiens waren die Portugiesen 1498 die ersten Händler zur See seit den Phöniziern, die das Kap umrundeten. Aber erst 154 Jahre später, als die Niederländer erste koloniale Wurzeln am Fuß des Berges schlugen, begann die Geschichte von Kapstadt.

Trotz unsicherer Anfangsjahre erwiesen sich die Siedler, die man mit dem Aufbau einer Versorgungsstation für den Segelverkehr zwischen Europa und den Ostindischen Inseln beauftragt hatte, als zäh. Die Niederländer hielten anderthalb Jahrhunderte lang ihren „Besitzanspruch" auf das Kap, und währenddessen wuchs dort eine Stadt. Rund um eine steinerne Festung und bunt zusammengewürfelte weiß getünchte, niedrige Gebäude erstreckte sich nun auch Ackerland. Man bepflanzte auch die ersten Weinberge, und es entstand eine unsichere Handelsbeziehung zu den einheimischen Hirten. Elegante Gebäude gaben der Siedlung langsam das Erscheinungsbild einer wohlhabenden Stadt. Und aus weit entfernten Kolonien wurden Sklaven als Arbeiter und Handwerker ans Kap deportiert.

Dann kamen die Briten und gaben der Stadt ihren kulturellen Anstrich. Kapstadt wurde noch bedeutender, als die europäischen Mächte ernsthaft um ihren Anteil an afrikanischem Grundbesitz und an den ober- wie unterirdischen Schätzen zu kämpfen begannen. Weit nördlich wurden Gold und Diamanten entdeckt, und die Kriege um die Gebietskontrollen endeten erst 1910 mit der Gründung des Staates Südafrika.

Zwar endete die britische Herrschaft am Kap, nicht aber die weiße Vormachtstellung. Sie erreichte ihren repressiven Höhepunkt während der Apartheidjahre des 20. Jahrhunderts. Aber selbst diese düstere Periode fand ihr willkommenes Ende, als Nelson Mandela nach 26 langen Jahren Gefängnishaft auf Robben Island vom Balkon des Rathauses seine Rede an die Nation hielt. Nach über drei Jahrhunderten weißer Unterdrückung bewegte sich das Land voller Hoffnung in eine ungewisse Zukunft.

Kapstadt war Zeuge all dessen. Überall erinnert etwas an die Vergangenheit – Kopfsteinpflaster, kapholländischer oder viktorianischer Stil, eine Sklavenglocke oder eine stattliche Eichenallee. Aber Kapstadt ist auch eine moderne Stadt mit zeitgenössischer Architektur, lebendigen Märkten, Einkaufszentren, Sportstadien, trendigen Hotels und Restaurants. Trotz tiefer sozialer und wirtschaftlicher Gräben und trotz der unbequemen Koexistenz eines reichen Kerns umgeben von wuchernden Slums, ist diese Stadt voller Leben, Enthusiasmus und Selbstbewusstsein, passend zu ihrer wachsenden Bedeutung als einem der Top-Reiseziele der Welt.

Quite when the first humans stood on the slopes of Table Mountain and gazed across the waters of the bay curling northwards from the plains below, is an occasion lost in time. The "oldest drawing in the world," is a 73,000-year-old pattern of lines drawn with an ochre crayon in a cave about 300 kilometres to the east of the city. And, some evidence suggests, the ancient Phoenicians reached these parts in their sail-powered gauloi 2,700 years ago.

Notwithstanding these ancient links, compared with the millennia-old capitals and settlements of northern Africa, Cape Town is a young city not even four centuries into its life. But it is the oldest in southern Africa, and its history is deeply rooted in the land and its people.

Spurred on by the search for a sea passage to the spice-rich shores of Asia, the Portuguese, in 1498, were the first maritime traders after the Phoenicians to round the Cape. But it wasn't until 154 years later when the Dutch put down early colonial roots at the foot of the mountain, that Cape Town was born.

The settlement's early years were tenuous. But the people charged with establishing a revictualling point for sailing vessels plying back and forth between Europe and the East Indies were a hardy bunch. The Dutch clung stubbornly to their "ownership" of the Cape for a century and a half, and during their tenure, a city began to grow. From a stone-walled castle and a motley collection of low, white-washed buildings, farmlands began to spread. Food was grown, the first vineyards were planted, and an uneasy trading relationship began with local herders. Elegant buildings began to give the settlement the air of a prosperous town. And slaves were deported from far away colonies to provide both labour and artisanal skills. Then came the British to add their cultural veneer, and the city burgeoned in importance as the European powers scrambled in earnest for their slice of Africa's real estate and the treasures that lay above and below the ground. Gold and diamonds were discovered far to the north and wars were fought over their control, ending, in 1910, with the birth of South Africa.

British rule might have ended at the Cape, but white supremacy remained, reaching its oppressive zenith in the apartheid years of the second half of the 1900s. But even this grim period came to a welcome end when Nelson Mandela, freed after 26 years in prison – much of it on Robben Island in Cape Town's bay – spoke to an awaiting nation from the balcony of the City Hall. More than three centuries of white domination had ended, and the country staggered uncertainly, but with hope, into the future.

Cape Town has been witness to it all. At almost every turn there is something – a cobbled street, an intricate Victorian detail, a Cape-Dutch façade, a slave bell, or an avenue of stately oaks to remind one of times past. But it is also a modern city of contemporary architecture, bustling markets, shopping malls, sports stadiums, trendy hotels and restaurants. And, notwithstanding deep social and economic divisions, and the uncomfortable reality of a wealthy core surrounded by sprawling slums, it is filled with vibrancy, enthusiasm and confidence befitting its growing status as one of the top city destinations in the world.

Vergangenheit & Zukunft ::: Past & Future

Alt und neu. *Links:* Das Treppenhaus zur Galerie der Groote Kerk (Afrikaans: Große Kirche) von Kapstadt, die 1841 gebaut wurde. Seit 1678 gibt es an dieser Stelle christliche Gottesdienste, und der Turm der ursprünglichen Kirche blieb als Teil des jetzigen Gebäudes erhalten. Die Orgel ist die größte des Landes. *Oben:* Das Zeitz Museum of Contemporary Art Africa (MOCAA) ist das größte Kunstmuseum in Afrika. Es widmet sich der Kunst Afrikas und seiner Diaspora. ::: Old and the new. *Left:* The staircase leading to the gallery of Cape Town's Groote Kerk which was built in 1841. The site has been a place of Christian worship since 1678, and the original tower remains part of the present building. The church also lays claim to being home to the country's largest organ which was installed in 1954. *Above:* The Zeitz Museum of Contemporary Art Africa (MOCAA) is the biggest art museum in Africa and is dedicated to presenting the art of Africa and its diaspora.

Landschaft land
sc
ape

An der südwestlichen Spitze des afrikanischen Kontinents stößt ein dünner, knotiger Landfinger trotzig in den Atlantischen Ozean vor. Von der Zeit und den Elementen geformt, ist dies ein Ort von atemberaubender Schönheit. Der Tafelberg mit seinen Begleitern Teufelsspitze und Lion's Head beherrscht eine der unverwechselbarsten Landschaften unseres Planeten. Und vor dieser dramatischen Kulisse liegt Kapstadt wie drapiert zwischen Sandsteinwällen und dem Meer. Eine Stadt, die scheinbar alles hat: imposante Berge, die mancherorts steil in den Ozean abfallen, Wälder, eine Flora von unübertroffener Vielfalt, blendend weiße Sandstrände und Weinberge, die manche der weltbesten Weine produzieren. ::: At the southwestern tip of the African continent, a thin, gnarled finger of land projects defiantly into the Atlantic Ocean. Sculpted by time and the elements, it is a place of breathtaking beauty. The focal point is Table Mountain which, with its cohorts of Devil's Peak and Lion's Head, forms one of the most iconic landscapes anywhere on the planet. And it is against this dramatic backdrop that the city of Cape Town lies draped between sandstone ramparts and the sea. Cape Town seems to have everything – imposing mountains that in places drop sheer into the ocean, forests, a floral diversity of unparalleled abundance, blindingly white crescent beaches, and vineyard mantled hills producing some of the finest wines in the world.

Hochebene & Tiefebene ::: High plain & Lowlands

Links: Der Blick von Signal Hill durch Kloof Nek – dem Landsattel zwischen Lion's Head und Tafelberg. Dahinter liegen die Zwölf Apostel (Twelve Apostles), eine zerklüftete Bergkette, die südwärts an Camps Bay vorbei bis Llandudno und Hout Bay reicht. *Oben:* Ein Fischer-Dingi, das bei Ebbe auf Sand gelaufen ist, in der Langebaan-Lagune an der Westküste, 130 Kilometer nördlich von Kapstadt. ::: *Left:* The view from Signal Hill through Kloof Nek – the saddle of land between Lion's Head and Table Mountain. The Twelve Apostles lie beyond, a craggy spine of mountains reaching southwards past Camps Bay towards Llandudno and Hout Bay. *Above:* Fishing dinghy stranded at low tide in Langebaan Lagoon on the West Coast, 130 kilometres north of Cape Town.

Eine einsame Windmühle steht Wache zwischen Nieuwoudtville und Loeriesfontein in der trockenen Naquamaland-Region nördlich von Kapstadt. Auf dem gewerblich und kommunal genutzten Land wird hauptsächlich Viehwirtschaft betrieben. ::: A lonely windmill stands sentinel between Nieuwoudtville and Loeriesfontein in the arid Namaqualand region north of Cape Town. Agriculture, mainly livestock, is the primary land use on commercial and communal farmlands.

Der Atlantic Beach Golfplatz bildet eine hellgrüne Schneise im niedrigen Buschwerk. Der Tafelberg, halb versteckt unter seinem „Tischtuch", liegt 35 Kilometer weiter südlich.
::: The Atlantic Beach golf links cut a bright green swathe in the low, scrubby bush. Table Mountain, half-hidden under its "tablecloth," lies 35 kilometres to the south.

Ein Fischerboot, hochgezogen ins Flachwasser der Langebaan-Lagune im West-Coast-Nationalpark. Dieser ist von Kapstadt aus ein beliebtes Ziel für Tagestouren.
::: A lone fishing boat hauled up in the shallows of Langebaan Lagoon, part of the West Coast National Park, a popular day-trip destination from Cape Town.

In einer Gegend, die für ihre Frühlingsblüte berühmt ist, leuchtet das Feld zwischen Nieuwoudtville und Calvinia durch die tief rosafarbenen Blütenköpfe der *Brunsvigia*, einer herbstblühenden Vertreterin der Amaryllis-Familie. ::: This field between the West Coast towns of Nieuwoudtville and Calvinia is alive with the deep pink crowns of *Brunsvigia*, an autumn-flowering member of the Amaryllis family.

Von einer Felsklippe aus beobachtet ein Paar den langsamen Aufstieg der Seilbahn zum Gipfel des Tafelbergs. Jedes Jahr machen mehr als eine Million Menschen diese kurze, aber spektakuläre Fahrt. ::: From a cliff edge on Table Mountain, a couple watches the slowly rotating cable car hauling tourists to the summit. More than a million people make the short but spectacular journey every year.

Rechts: Der leuchtend weiße Sand von Dias Beach, gesehen vom Ausguck am Cape Point. Der Strand ist benannt nach dem portugiesischen Entdecker und Edelmann Bartolomeu Dias, der 1488 als erster Europäer das Kap umrundete.
::: *Right:* The pearly-white sands of Dias Beach from the lookout at Cape Point. The stretch of sand is named after the Portuguese nobleman and explorer Bartolomeu Dias, who in 1488 was the first European to round the Cape.

Oben: Es schneit selten in Kapstadt, und auch dann liegt nur ein Hauch von Weiß auf den Berggipfeln. Im Inland jedoch gibt es gelegentlich heftige Schneefälle. *Links:* Watt nördlich von Kapstadt. :::
Above: Snow rarely comes to Cape Town, and then only as a light mountain-top dusting. Inland farms and towns, however, occasionally experience heavy falls. *Left:* Tidal mudflats north of Cape Town.

Hochebene & Tiefebene ::: High plain & Lowlands   29

Stadt & Land ::: Town & Rural

Links: Morgendliche Ruhe vor dem täglichen Verkehrsgewimmel auf der Heerengracht. Der Name dieser Hauptverkehrsader der City bedeutet im Niederländischen „Herrenkanal" und verweist auf den Wasserweg, der früher an dieser Straße entlanglief. Bis in die 1860er-Jahre prägte ein aus den Bergen gespeistes Kanalnetz die Stadt. *Oben:* Ein einsamer Reiter am Noordhoek-Strand, der sich 8,5 Kilometer ohne Unterbrechung von Chapman's Peak bis nach Kommetje hinzieht. ::: *Left:* Early morning quiet before the daily bustle of traffic along the Heerengracht, the city's main downtown thoroughfare. The name derives from a Dutch word meaning "Gentlemans' Canal," a reference to the watercourse that once ran along its length. A network of mountain-fed canals was a feature of Cape Town until the 1860s. *Above:* Deserted but for a lone rider, the Noordhoek beach stretches an uninterrupted 8.5 kilometres from Chapman's Peak to the village of Kommetjie.

32 Stadt & Land ::: Town & Rural

City Bowl, Waterfront und Hafen im letzten Abendlicht. Ein schmales Band aus Vorort-Lichtern lässt auch noch den Nordrand der Tafelbucht erkennen. :::
The last light of dusk as night settles over the City Bowl, waterfront and harbour. A thin band of suburban lights marks the northern fringe of Table Bay.

Oben: Ein Privathaus am Hang des Lion's Head. *Darunter rechts:* Konzert im De-Waal-Park. *Links:* Das Einkaufszentrum in der V&A Waterfront an Südafrikas ältestem Hafen zieht jährlich mehr als 23 Millionen Besucher an. ::: *Top:* A private home on the slopes of Lion's Head. *Below right:* Concert in De Waal Park. *Left:* The shopping mall at the V&A Waterfront in South Africa's oldest working harbour attracts more than 23 million visitors a year.

Blick von den Weinbergen des Vergelegen-Guts auf die Stadt Somerset West und die Küste der False Bay. Vergelegen, einer der ältesten Höfe am Western Cape, wurde um 1700 vom damals niederländischen Gouverneur des Kaps, Willem Adriaan van der Stel, zum ersten Mal besiedelt. ::: The view from the vineyards of the Vergelegen Estate towards the town of Somerset West and the False Bay coast. Vergelegen, one of the oldest farms in the Western Cape, was first settled in 1700 by the then Dutch Governor of the Cape Willem Adriaan van der Stel.

Land & Meer ::: Land & Sea

Links: Die streng angelegten Weinreben des Diemersdal-Guts fließen wie Wellen über die Hügel der Durbanville-Weingegend nördlich von Kapstadt. *Oben:* Eine sturmgepeitschte See verschlingt förmlich die Hafenmauer von Kalk Bay an der Küste der False Bay. Solche enormen Wellen treten im tiefen Winter auf. Ansonsten ist das bescheidene, bunte Fischerdorf eher ein Hort der Ruhe. ::: *Left:* The regimented rows of Diemersdal Estate flow wave-like across the Durbanville Hills wine region to the north of Cape Town. *Above:* A storm-driven sea engulfs the habour wall at Kalk Bay along the False Bay coast. Such enormous waves are a feature of the deep winter months. For the most part, an air of tranquillity mantles this quaint and colourful fishing haven.

Sonnenaufgang über den Weingärten von Klein Constantia, die sich in den kühlen oberen Lagen am Fuß des Constantiabergs hinziehen. Das Gut existiert seit 1685 und bringt unter anderem Spitzenweine wie den Vin de Constance hervor, der im Stil der einst in Europa gefeierten, legendären süßen Weine des Tals wieder produziert wird. ::: Sunrise over the Klein Constantia vineyards, which lie along the cool upper foothills of the Constantiaberg. The estate dates back to 1685 and produces some of South Africa's top wines, including Vin de Constance, recreated in the style of valley's legendary sweet wines much celebrated in 18th- and 19th-century Europe.

Ländliches Stellenbosch. *Oben:* Ernte frühmorgens auf dem Rust-en-Vrede-Gut. *Links:* Eine Königsprotea auf dem Weingut Blaauwklippen. Ein Blick über die Blaauwklippen-Weingärten von der benachbarten Keermont Farm. ::: Rural Stellenbosch. *Top:* Early morning harvesting at Rust-en-Vrede Estate. *Left:* A king protea on the Blaauwklippen Wine Estate. *Above:* The view over the Blaauwklippen vineyards from the adjacent Keermont Farm.

An einem späten Sommerabend schimmern die Wolken im rosigen Widerschein des Sonnenuntergangs. Es herrscht Ebbe, und ein einzelner Angler versucht sein Glück im nicht gerade ruhigen Ozean. ::: A late summer evening and the afterglow of sunset paints the sky with sweeps of pink and mauve. The tide is out, and a lone fisherman tries his luck in the all-but waveless ocean.

Einheimische wie Touristen lieben die Kolonie bedrohter Brillenpinguine in Boulders Beach bei Simon's Town an der Küste der False Bay. Wegen ihres eselähnlichen Rufs nannte man die Vögel früher Jackass-Pinguine (jackass, Engl.: Eselhengst, grober Kerl). Diese einzige frei lebende afrikanische Pinguin-Art findet man nur entlang der südafrikanischen Küste. ::: The colony of endangered African penguins at Boulders Beach near Simon's Town on the False Bay coast, is a firm favourite with locals and visitors alike. Once known as the Jackass penguin because of its donkey-like braying call, the species is the continent's only indigenous penguin, and it is only found along the coastline of southern Africa.

Unten: Frühmorgens in den Swartland-Weingärten nahe der Stadt Malmesbury. In der Ferne ist der Tafelberg sichtbar. *Rechts:* Die Kap-Walroute erstreckt sich von der False Bay bis zur Plettenberg Bay im Osten. Diese fast 1.000 Kilometer lange Strecke bietet manche der besten Stellen zur Walbeobachtung weltweit, besonders in der Hauptkalbzeit von August bis Oktober. ::: *Below:* Early morning in the Swartland vineyards near the town of Malmesbury. Table Mountain is visible in the far distance. *Right:* The Cape Whale Route extends from False Bay through to Plettenberg Bay in the east. The nearly 1.000-kilometre stretch is one of the best whale-watching destinations in the world, especially in the peak calving months of August through to October.

Links: Der Zauber des südlichen Himmels bei Nacht. *Unten:* Gemeine Delfine in Höchstgeschwindigkeit vor Kapstadts Atlantikufer. Diese extrem aktiven, schnellen Delfine bewegen sich oft in großen Schulen von hundert oder mehr Tieren. :::
Left: The magic of the southern skies at night. *Below:* A pod of common dolphins moves at top speed off Cape Town's Atlantic seaboard. These extremely active, fast-moving dolphins are often found in large groups of a hundred or more.

Delaire ::: Delaire

Ein Skulpturen-Paar von Dylan Lewis in den exquisit gestalteten Gärten des Delaire-Graff-Guts am Stadtrand von Stellenbosch. Das Anwesen entstand nach Entwürfen seines Besitzers Laurence Graff und öffnete 2009. Graff gehört zu den weltweit führenden Diamantenproduzenten, ist außerdem ein Philantrop und ein eifriger Sammler moderner Kunst. ::: Paired Dylan Lewis sculptures add to the drama of the exquisitely landscaped gardens of the Delaire Graff Estate on the outskirts of Stellenbosch. The estate opened in 2009 and is the brainchild of the owner, Laurence Graff, a world leader within in the diamond industry, philanthropist, and an avid collector of modern and contemporary art.

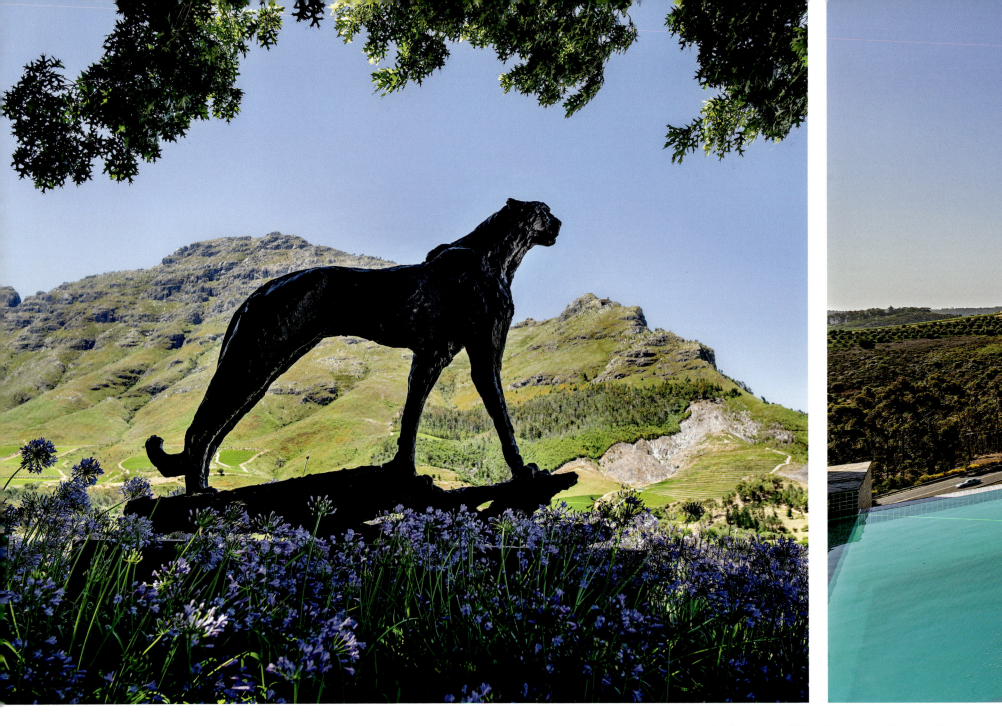

Die wilde, ungezähmte Schönheit eines Dylan-Lewis-Geparden im Kontrast zu den klaren Linien des Pooldecks in der Delaire-Graff-Lodge. ::: The wild, untamed beauty of a Dylan Lewis cheetah contrasts with the manicured formality of the pool deck at the Delaire Graff Lodge.

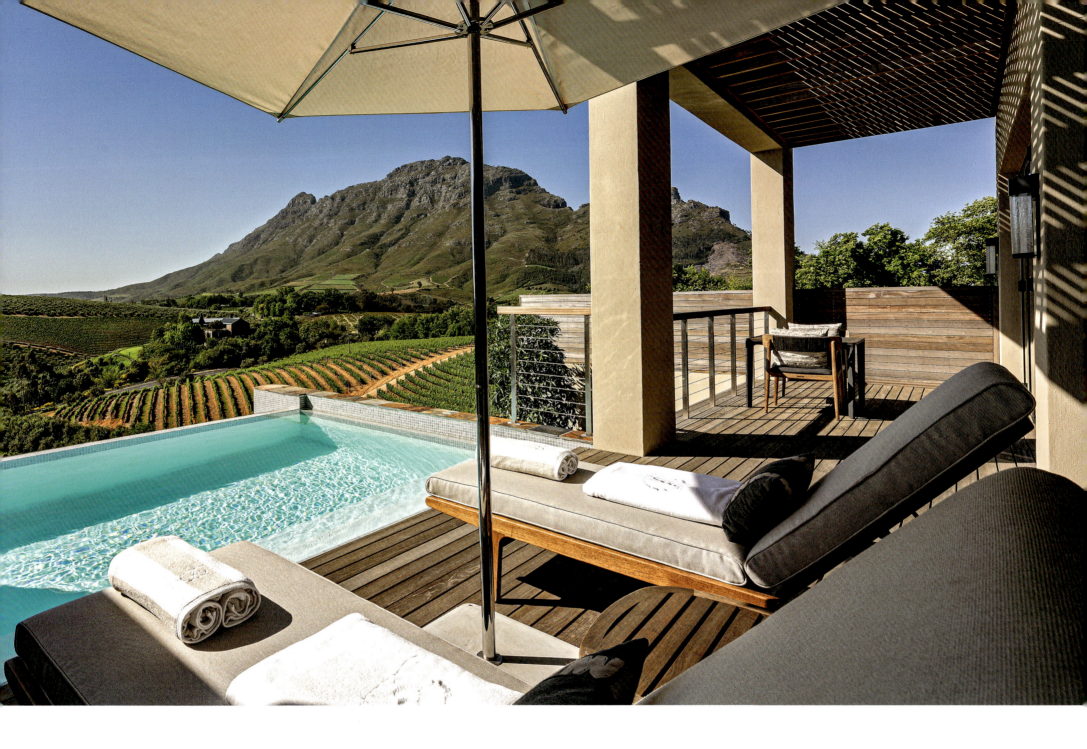

Die gesamte Anlage der Delaire-Graff-Lodge, hoch oben in den Hügeln über Stellenbosch, ist von Kunst durchdrungen. Diese spiegelt sich in den wunderbar ausgeklügelten Menüs, in den Weinen ihrer Restaurants, in der Architektur wider, und natürlich in den Bildern und Skulpturen, die jeden Raum schmücken. ::: Art permeates the entire environment of the Delaire Graff Lodge, set high in the hills above Stellenbosch. It manifests as much in the beautifully conceived and executed menus of its restaurants, the wines of the estate, the architecture, and of course the paintings and sculptures adorning every room. :::

Atlantik & Indischer Ozean ::: Atlantic & Indian Ocean

Links: Düstere Sturmwolken ziehen über dem Vorort Sea Point und einer zu Schaum gepeitschten See herauf. *Oben:* Der Leuchtturm von Cape Agulhas, etwa 250 Kilometer östlich von Cape Point, der schroffen Spitze der Kap-Halbinsel, die oft fälschlich als die südlichste Spitze Afrikas bezeichnet wird. Diese Ehre fällt tatsächlich Agulhas zu, wo der Kontinent ganz undramatisch in einer Reihe von trügerischen, flachen Riffen in den Ozean abfällt, die über die Jahrhunderte so manchem Schiff zum Grab geworden sind.
::: *Left:* Angry storm clouds loom above the suburb of Sea Point and a sea whipped into a froth of spume. *Above:* The lighthouse at Cape Agulhas, some 250 kilometres east of Cape Point, the rugged tip of the Cape Peninsula, which is often mistakenly referenced as Africa's southernmost point. That honour actually belongs to Agulhas, where the continent slides rather undramatically into the ocean in a series of treacherous, shallow reefs that have been the grave of many vessels over the centuries.

Die farbenfrohen Badehütten in Muizenberg an der False Bay wecken zunächst Erinnerungen an das Viktorianische Zeitalter. Muizenberg war aber auch Schauplatz der Schlacht, welche 1795 die niederländische Herrschaft am Kap beendete und die britische Dominanz über das südliche Afrika mit sich brachte. Einst ein vornehmer Badeort, ist das heutige Muizenberg besser bekannt als ein Top-Surfrevier und für seinen kosmopolitischen und unkonventionellen Lebensstil. ::: Redolent of the Cape's Victorian era, a regimented row of colourfully painted beach huts lines the beach at Muizenberg on the False Bay coast. The suburb marks the site of 1795 battle which ended Dutch rule at the Cape and saw the beginning of British domination of southern Africa. Once a resort town for the rich and famous, contemporary Muizenberg is better known as a top surfing destination and its far more bohemian and cosmopolitan lifestyle.

Hochbetrieb auf der Restaurant- und Hotelmeile von Camps Bay. Dieser reiche, kosmopolitische Vorort liegt unterhalb der Zwölf Apostel, die als Teil der Tafelberg-Kette vom Massiv oberhalb der Stadt nach Süden bis Cape Point weiterlaufen. Das Gebiet ist benannt nach Friedrich von Kamptz, einem deutschen Matrosen, der sich hier im späten 18. Jahrhundert niederließ und die Witwe Anna Wernich heiratete, die den Hof an der Bucht besaß. ::: Camps Bay's bustling strip of cheek-by-jowl restaurants and hotels. The affluent and cosmopolitan suburb lies beneath the watchful gaze of the Twelve Apostles, part of the Table Mountain range extending from the massif above the city southwards to Cape Point. The area was originally named after Friedrich von Kamptz, a German sailor who settled in the Cape in the late 1700s and married the widow Anna Wernich who owned the farm adjoining the bay.

Unten: Wintersturm-Wolken über Hout Bay. *Darunter links:* Blick nach Süden über die Atlantikküste der Halbinsel bis Cape Point. *Darunter rechts:* Beim Angeln an der Einfahrt zur Wohnsiedlung V&A Marina (Engl.: Yachthafen). ::: *Below:* Winter storm clouds over Hout Bay. *Bottom left:* The Peninsula's Atlantic seaboard, looking south towards Cape Point in the far distance. *Bottom right:* Fishing off the entrance to the V&A Marina development.

Der Yachthafen-Komplex liegt im Zentrum der quirligen V&A-Waterfront-Siedlung. Kapstadts historische Docklands rund um die Victoria and Alfred Basins wurden in den späten 1980er-Jahren mit einem Fokus auf Geschäfte, Tourismus und urbanes Wohnen neu konzipiert. Der Rest ist, wie man sagt, Geschichte. ::: The yacht marina complex lies at the heart of the vibrant V&A Waterfront development. Cape Town's historic docklands around the Victoria and Alfred Basins began a new lease on life in the late 1980s as a focus of retail, tourism and residential development. The rest, as they say, is history.

Kleinood ::: **Kleinood**

Besucher genießen ein mittägliches Festmahl auf der Kleinood-Wein-Farm im Blaauwklippen Valley am Fuß des Stellenbosch Mountain. Der Name bezeichnet auf Afrikaans etwas Kleines, Kostbares und passt sehr schön zu diesem bezaubernden Gut. Gerard de Villiers, Spross einer Hugenottenfamilie in elfter Generation und seine Frau Libby entdeckten dieses friedliche Eckchen der Kap-Weinregion im Jahr 2000 und entschieden sich, hier ihr Heim einzurichten. ::: Visitors enjoy a lunchtime feast at the Kleinood wine farm, which lies in the Blaauwklippen Valley at the foot of the Stellenbosch Mountain. Kleinood means something small and precious in Afrikaans, an apt name for this charming estate so treasured by Gerard de Villiers, the 11th generation scion of a French Huguenot family, and his wife Libby. They found this tranquil corner of the Cape Winelands in 2000 and decided to make it their home.

Natur, Weinherstellung, ein Olivenhain und die Gärten ergeben ein harmonisches Ganzes auf Kleinood, wo die Liebe zum Detail ein Markenzeichen aller Produkte ist. Sogar die Weinetiketten, deren Design sich vom Familienwappen ableitet, werden auf handgemachtem Papier gedruckt, von Hand in Form gerissen und einzeln auf jede Flasche geklebt. :::
Nature, winemaking, an olive grove and gardens combine in a harmonious whole at Kleinood, where meticulous attention to detail is the hallmark of everything produced. Even the wine labels, their design derived from the de Villiers family crest, are hand-printed on hand-made paper, hand-torn to size and individually pasted onto each bottle.

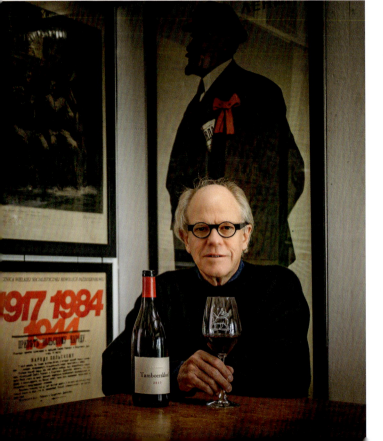

Kleinoods Rosengarten und der Blick in die Weingärten, in denen Syrah und etwas Mourvèdre angebaut wird. Das berufliche Interesse des Ingenieurs Gerard de Villiers *(links)* reicht weit über sein eigenes Gut hinaus – er hat viele Kellereien entworfen und gebaut, sowohl für viele bekannte südafrikanische Marken als auch in Großbritannien, Frankreich, den USA und in Israel.

::: Kleinood's rose garden and the view into vineyards planted with Syrah and a small block of Mourvèdre. Engineer Gerard de Villiers' *(left)* professional interest in winemaking extends well beyond his own estate – he has designed and built wine cellars for many notable South African brands, as well as across Britain, France, and the United States and Israel.

Santa Anna's ::: Santa Anna's

Das verschlafene Städtchen Gordon's Bay liegt im östlichen Winkel der False Bay, ungefähr 50 Kilometer vom Zentrum Kapstadts entfernt. Hier befindet sich das Kleinod Santa Anna's, ein kleiner Betrieb, in dem vier original südafrikanische „Amigos" *(rechts, oben)* mexikanisch inspirierte Köstlichkeiten herstellen. Ihre Tortillas, Tortilla-Chips und Salsas bestehen alle aus glutenfreien Bio-Zutaten ohne Gentechnik, wo immer möglich aus lokalem Anbau. Kapstadt auf mexikanisch serviert! ::: The sleepy town of Gordon's Bay is located at the eastern corner of False Bay, about 50 kilometres from the centre of Cape Town. Here you will find the jewel Santa Anna's, a small factory where four home-grown South African "amigos" *(right, above)* make authentic Mexican-style delicacies. Their tortillas, tortilla chips, and salsas are all from naturally gluten free, non-GMO, organic ingredients, sourced locally wherever possible. Cape Town served up Mexican style!

Festland & Inseln ::: Mainland & Islands

Links: Die Kap-Halbinsel in voller Länge, mit der Ostseite des Tafelbergs und der Teufelsspitze am Horizont. *Oben:* Die dunkle Geschichte von Robben Island als Strafkolonie umfasst mehr als drei Jahrhunderte. Ab den frühen 1960er-Jahren erlangte die Insel als Gefangenenlager für die politischen Häftlinge des Apartheidregimes 30 Jahre lang international traurige Berühmtheit. Ihr bekanntester Insasse war Nelson Mandela. Heute ist die Insel eine Welterbestätte und dient als nationale Gedenkstätte. ::: *Left:* The full sweep of the Cape Peninsula with the eastern face of Table Mountain and devil's Peak in the far distance. *Above:* Robben Island's dark history as a penal colony spanned more than three centuries. For 30 years from the early 1960s, the island achieved international notoriety as a place of incarceration for political prisoners of the South Africa's apartheid regime. Its most celebrated inmate was, of course, the late Nelson Mandela. Now a World Heritage site, the island serves as a living museum.

Sonnenuntergänge am Kap sind oft spektakulär: Meer, Land und Himmel baden in Mustern aus Gold, Purpur und jeder Farbe dazwischen. Sonnenuntergang über Tsaarbank im West Coast National Park nördlich von Kapstadt. ::: Sunsets at the Cape are frequently spectacular events, bathing the sea, land and sky in patterns of gold, crimson and every shade in between. Sunset over Tsaarbank in the West Coast National Park north of Cape Town.

Natur & Kulturlandschaft ::: Nature & Cultural Landscape

Gegenüberliegende Seite: Wie ein frühlingsfarbener Teppich breiten sich blühende Watsonien über die unteren Hänge des Tafelbergs. Rings um Kapstadt feiert die Natur das Ende der kalten, feuchten Wintermonate mit gelben und rosafarbenen Wildblumen. *Oben:* Die raue Form- und Farbgebung der Dylan-Lewis-Skulptur spiegelt die wilden Konturen und Schattierungen der zerklüfteten Hügel im Hintergrund. ::: *Opposite page:* Watsonias bloom in a carpet of spring colour stretching up the lower slopes of Table Mountain. Almost everywhere there is open ground around Cape Town, nature celebrates the end of the cold, wet months of winter with swathes of yellow and pink wildflowers. *Above:* The rough colour and form of a Dylan Lewis sculpture echo the wild contours and hue of the rugged peaks beyond.

Gegenüberliegende Seite. Oben: Der weltberühmte Botanische Garten Kirstenbosch am Osthang des Tafelbergs. *Unten:* Der Dylan Lewis Sculpture Garden in Stellenbosch. *Oben:* Sonnenlicht fällt durch die Bäume des Tokai Forest, eines beliebten Ausflugsziels für Picknicks, Mountainbiking und Spaziergänge. ::: *Opposite page. Top:* The world-renowned Kirstenbosch Botanical Gardens on the eastern slopes of Table Mountain. *Below:* The Dylan Lewis Sculpture Garden in Stellenbosch. *Above:* Sunlight filters through the trees of the Tokai Forest, a favourite southern suburbs spot for picnics, mountain biking and walks.

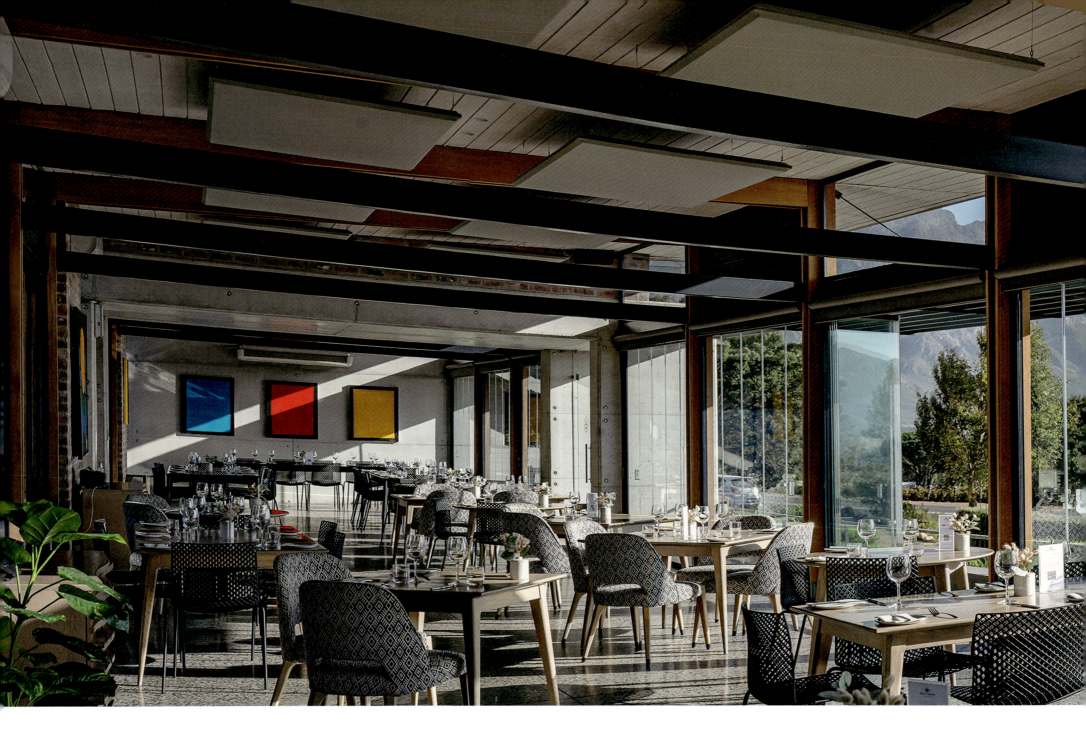

Haute Cabrière ::: Haute Cabrière

Die Panorama-Terrasse des Haute Cabrière: Seine Glasfront erlaubt einen ungehinderten Blick auf das atemberaubende Franschhoek-Tal, etwa 80 Kilometer von Kapstadt entfernt. Die Geschichte des Guts reicht über drei Jahrhunderte zurück bis ins Jahr 1694, als der Hugenotte Pierre Jourdan sich in der französischen Ecke der jungen niederländischen Kolonie ansiedelte. Sein Name findet ein Echo in der Hausspezialität, den Cap-Classique-Weinen. Das Gut ist seit 1982 im Besitz der Familie von Arnim. ::: The glass-fronted terrace restaurant at Haute Cabrière with its uninterrupted views across the breathtakingly beautiful Franschhoek Valley, some 80 kilometres from Cape Town. The estate's history stretches back across three centuries when, in 1694, Huguenot Pierre Jourdan settled in the "French Corner" of the fledgling Dutch colony at the Cape. His name echoes in Haute Cabriere's signature Cap Classique wines produced by the von Arnim family, who have owned the estate since 1982.

Hoch oben auf dem Franschhoek-Pass gelegen, ist Haute Cabrière von Bergen umgeben, die in vorzeitlichen geologischen Umbrüchen entstanden sind. Auf diesem einzigartigen Terroir führt Takuan von Arnim, Haute Cabrières Kellermeister der zweiten Generation, die Produktion von Spitzenweinen fort. Hier demonstriert er das Öffnen einer Sektflasche per Säbel, ein Brauch aus napoleonischer Zeit. ::: Perched high on the Franschhoek Pass, Haute Cabrière is surrounded by mountains formed during ancient geological upheavals. In this unique terroir, Takuan von Arnim, Haute Cabriere's second-generation cellar master, continues the family legacy of growing fine wines. Here he demonstrates the art of opening a champagne bottle with a sabre, a tradition begun in Napoleonic times.

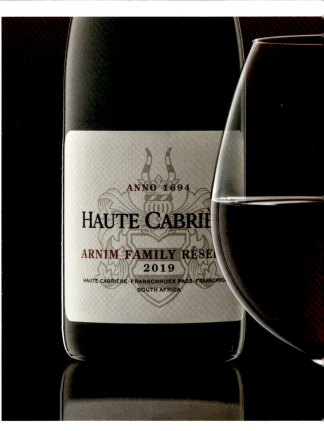

Ein freundlicher, warmherziger Geist und die einladende Stimmung sind typisch für das Gut Haute Cabrière. Es ist ein echter Familienbetrieb. Gründer Achim von Arnim *(oben rechts)* ist eine der großen Persönlichkeiten der Kap-Weinregion, und hier genießt er die Früchte seiner Arbeit zusammen mit seiner Frau Hildegard und zwei von ihren Kindern, Tanja und Kellermeister Takuan. ::: A spirit of friendliness, warmth and a pervading sense of welcome is the hallmark of the Haute Cabrière estate. It truly is a family affair. Founder, Achim von Arnim *(top right)*, is undisputedly one of the great personalities of the Cape Winelands, and here he enjoys the fruits of his labours with his wife, Hildegard, and two of their offspring, Tanja and cellar master Takuan.

Geselligkeit, Wein und gutes Essen stehen im Zentrum des Haute Cabrière Restaurant & Terrace. Dort weben gefeierte Köche an ihrer kulinarischen Magie. Sie legen großen Wert auf regionale und saisonale Zutaten, die aus ökologischem Anbau stammen. ::: Conviviality, wine and good food are the essential experiences at the Haute Cabrière Restaurant & Terrace, where renowned chefs weave their culinary magic. The menu of classic dishes is strongly focussed on seasonal ingredients, locally grown and organically farmed.

Gesellschaft society

Kapstadt ist ein vielschichtiger Mix aus Menschen mit religiösen, sprachlichen und kulturellen Wurzeln in Afrika, Europa und Asien. Einerseits reich und kultiviert wie viele Städte der Alten Welt, kämpfen in Kapstadt andererseits Gemeinden um die grundlegendsten Einrichtungen und Dienstleistungen. Diese Spaltung zwischen Privilegien und Elend tritt oft krass zutage in einer Stadt, die noch mit ihrer Vergangenheit ins Reine kommen muss. Trotz aller Herausforderungen sprüht die „Mother City", wie sie liebevoll genannt wird, unbestreitbar vor kreativer und kultureller Energie. Das ist überall dort spürbar, wo neue Wege für eine gerechtere Teilhabe und eine erfolgreichere Zukunft für alle viereinhalb Millionen Einwohner beschritten werden. ::: Cape Town is a complex, layered mix of people, their languages, religion and backgrounds rooted in Africa, Europe and the East. At one level it is as wealthy and sophisticated as any Old-World city, but on the other, there is the depressing reality of communities battling for the very basic of amenities and services. This social divide between privilege and squalor is often starkly and uncomfortably revealed in a city still coming to terms with its past. However, for all its challenges, the Mother City, as Cape Town is fondly known, has an undeniable creative and cultural energy. It is palpable as new paths are explored towards a more inclusive and more prosperous future for all of its four-and-a-half million citizens.

Schwarz & Weiß ::: **Black & White**

Gegenüberliegende Seite: Ein Fotograf bei der Arbeit in seinem improvisierten Atelier – einem umgebauten Schiffscontainer – in der Cape Flats Township Khayelitsha. Mehr als eine Million Menschen leben hier dicht an dicht in einem der größten Slums der Welt. *Oben:* Zwanglos-ländliche Gemütlichkeit im Goatshed Restaurant in Fairview, einem Gut bei Paarl, bekannt für seine handwerklichen Produkte, besonders feinen Wein und Käse. ::: *Opposite page:* A photographer at work in his makeshift studio – a converted cargo container – in the Cape Flats township of Khayelitsha. More than a million people live in the cheek-by-jowl shacks of this sprawling suburb, one of the largest slums in the world. *Above:* The casual comfort of country-style hospitality of the Goatshed Restaurant at Fairview, an estate near Paarl, renowned for its artisanal produce focussed on fine wine and cheese.

Ganz oben: Ein Handwerksprojekt der Gemeinde in Langa, der ältesten Township von Kapstadt, früher ein Zentrum großen Widerstands gegen das Apartheidregime. *Oben:* Stand eines Handwerkers an der V&A Waterfront. Zwangloser Handel ist in Kapstadt, wie überall in Afrika, ein lebendiger Wirtschaftszweig und eine Chance für viele arbeitslose Firmengründer. ::: *Top:* A community craft project in Langa, the oldest of Cape Town's townships and formerly a centre of great resistance against the apartheid regime. *Above:* A craft seller at the V&A Waterfront. Informal trading in Cape Town, as elsewhere in South Africa, is a vibrant sector of the economy providing opportunities to many unemployed entrepreneurs.

The Crypt, in St. George's Cathedral im Herzen der Stadt, ist einer von Kapstadts vielen Jazzkellern. In der Mother City floriert Musik aller Stilrichtungen, in Konzerthallen, Freiluft-Amphitheatern, mondänen Clubs oder schmuddeligen Bars, in Cafés oder an Straßenecken. Egal, wonach Ihnen ist, Sie brauchen nie lange danach zu suchen. ::: The Crypt, at St. George's Cathedral in the heart of the city, is one of Cape Town's many live jazz hotspots. Music of all genres thrives in the Mother City across venues from concert halls, open-air amphitheatres, and sophisticated clubs to dingy bars, cafes and street corners. Whatever your mood and taste, you won't have to venture far to find it.

Arm & Reich ::: Poor & Rich

Gegensätzliche Lebenswelten. *Links:* Eine junge Frau füttert ihr Kind in einer baufälligen Hütte in Khayelitsha. *Oben:* Ein Luxus-Boutique-Hotel im teuren Vorort Camps Bay. Die junge Demokratie des Landes mag allen Bürgern politische Freiheit beschert haben, aber extreme Armut bleibt für viele immer noch eine tägliche Herausforderung. Traurigerweise hat Südafrika den zweifelhaften Ruf, die unausgewogenste Wirtschaft der Welt zu sein. ::: Contrasting lifestyles. *Left:* A young woman feeds her child in a tumbledown shack in Khayelitsha. *Above:* A luxury boutique hotel in the upmarket suburb of Camps Bay. The country's young democracy may have delivered political freedom for all its citizens, but the harsh realities of extreme poverty remain the day-to-day challenge for many. Sadly, South Africa has the dubious reputation of being the world's most unequal economy.

Aussicht über die Cape Flats in Richtung Stellenbosch und Somerset West. Man kann sich kaum vorstellen, dass dieser niedrig gelegene Landstrich, der die Kap-Halbinsel mit dem Hinterland verbindet, noch bis Mitte des 20. Jahrhunderts ein kaum bewohntes, sandiges Ödland war. In wenig mehr als einer Generation hat sich die Landschaft in ein Zuhause für Millionen größtenteils sehr armer Menschen verwandelt. ::: The view from a vantage point looking across the Cape Flats towards Stellenbosch and Somerset West. It is hard to imagine that as recently as the mid-1900s this low-lying stretch of land joining the Cape Peninsula with its hinterland was an all-but uninhabited sandy wasteland. In little more than a generation, the landscape has been transformed into the home of millions of mostly very poor people.

Gegenüberliegende Seite. Oben und unten rechts: Tshisanyama, buchstäblich „Fleisch verbrennen", sind Plätze, wo Township-Bewohner sich treffen, um über offenem Feuer zu grillen. Vielfach nur einfache Räumlichkeiten für Metzgereikunden, sind manche inzwischen beliebte Imbisse bei Einheimischen und Touristen. Mzoli's zum Beispiel, im Vorort Gugulethu, hat sich zur Wochenend-Institution entwickelt, wo man früh kommen muss, um noch einen Tisch zu ergattern. *Ganz links. Unten:* Ein Handwerker in Khayelitsha. *Oben:* Ein ruhiges Krocket-Spiel. :::
Opposite page. Top & bottom right: Tshisanyama, literally meaning to "burn meat", are places where township people gather to grill meat over an open fire. Often simple facilities for the convenience of a butcher's customers, many have become popular eateries for locals and tourists. Mzoli's, for example, in the suburb of Gugulethu has become something of a weekend institution where early arrival is essential if you are to get a table. *Far left. Below:* A craftsman at work in a Khayelitsha shop. *Above:* A quiet game of croquet.

Els & Co. ::: **Els & Co.**

Die alte Molkerei auf dem berühmten Rustenberg-Weingut am Rand von Stellenbosch bildet den Rahmen für ein außergewöhnliches Unternehmen. Els & Co. beschwört eine vergangene Epoche voller Stolz und Leidenschaft herauf und belebt die Kunst der Lederverarbeitung neu. Die exquisit handgearbeiteten Accessoires werden für anspruchsvolle Outdoor-Fans weltweit maßgeschneidert. ::: The old dairy on the renowned Rustenberg wine estate on the outskirts of Stellenbosch is the unexpected setting for an extraordinary entrepreneurial venture. Els & Co. invokes a bygone era of pride and passion, reviving the lost art of leatherworking in creating a range of bespoke, exquisitely hand-crafted accessories for discerning outdoor enthusiasts around the world.

Gemeinschaftlicher Aufschwung ist ein Kernanliegen von Ivan Volschenk, dem Gründer von Els & Co. Er stellt nur Frauen aus einem nahen Dorf ein und investiert mehrere Jahre in deren Ausbildung bis zum höchsten handwerklichen Standard. Jedes Produkt wird durch eine einzige Handwerkerin hergestellt und zum Schluss stolz mit ihren Initialen geprägt. ::: Community upliftment is a core value for Ivan Volschenk, Els & Co.'s founder. Only women from a nearby village are employed, and several years are invested in developing their skills to meet the highest standard of workmanship. Each product is made from start to finish by an individual craftswoman and proudly embossed with her initials.

Kultur culture

Kapstadt ist zweifellos ein atemberaubend schöner Ort. Aber um wirklich bedeutend zu sein, braucht eine Stadt mehr als gutes Aussehen. Es muss ein besonderer Sinn im Leben, bei Arbeit und Freizeit spürbar sein, ein anhaltendes Gefühl von Faszination, Entdeckerfreude und Bereicherung. Kapstadt besitzt dies im Übermaß. Schon allein die Berge und das Meer laden zum Entspannen und Erkunden ein. Wunderbare Gebäude, Museen und kulturelle Wahrzeichen wecken die Neugier auf Vergangenheit, Gegenwart und Zukunft der Stadt. Aber am besten zeigt sich der Geist von Kapstadt in seiner lebenssprühenden Kultur, in Musik, Essen und Trinken, Kunst und Handwerk. Wenn Sie über die geschäftigen Märkte bummeln, sich in einem Café entspannen, im Park von Kirstenbosch umherwandern und eine Auszeit in den Weingärten nehmen, dann wird der Geist von Kapstadt Sie umarmen. ::: Cape Town is a breathtakingly beautiful place, there is no denying that, but a city has to have more than physical attributes to be truly great. There has to be an added purpose to living, working and playing there, a pervading sense of intrigue, of discovery and enrichment. Cape Town has these in abundance. The mountains and the sea alone are invitations to unwind and explore. And there are exquisite buildings, museums and cultural landmarks to draw you into the city's the past, present and future. But above all, there is a vibrant popular culture embracing music, food and wine, arts and crafts. Together, these embody the spirit of Cape Town. And as you browse in the bustling markets, relax in a coffee shop, stroll in the manicured gardens of Kirstenbosch, and take time out in the vineyards, the spirit of Cape Town will embrace you.

Streetfood & Gastronomie ::: Streetfood & Gastronomy

Gegenüberliegende Seite: Kochfeuer für die Armen brennen die ganze Nacht über während des Ramadan, einem Monat des Fastens, Betens, Nachdenkens und der sozialen Fürsorge in muslimischen Gemeinden rund um die Welt. Der Ramadan in Kapstadt umfasst zahlreiche Traditionen, zum Beispiel wird dafür gesorgt, dass mittellose Familien ihr Fasten mit einer nahrhaften Mahlzeit brechen können. *Oben:* Im Gâte-Restaurant des Quoin-Rock-Weinguts wird angerichtet – Gourmetkultur auf neuen Höhen der Spitzenleistung. ::: *Opposite page:* Fires burn through the night as food is prepared for the poor during Ramadan, a month of fasting, prayer, reflection and social support in Muslim communities around the world. Ramadan in Cape Town embraces many special traditions, one of which is ensuring that destitute families are able to break their fast with a nutritious meal. *Above:* Plating food at Gâte, the Quoin Rock Estate's restaurant where the experience of fine dining is taken to new levels of excellence.

Gegenüberliegende Seite. Oben: Reife Feigen auf einem Markt in Kapstadt. *Darunter links:* Streetfood in Khayelitsha. *Unten rechts:* Ein Diamant wird bei Prins und Prins begutachtet, einer Goldschmiede für exquisiten Diamantenschmuck nach Maß. *Oben:* Gewusel auf dem Oranjezicht City Farm Market im historischen Granger-Bay-Distrikt an der V&A Waterfront. Hier bieten unabhängige örtliche Bauern und Handwerker ihren Waren an und begeistern mit einen neuen, frischen Blick auf Biolebensmittel und Bioküche. ::: *Opposite page. Top:* Ripe figs on offer in a Cape Town market. *Below left:* Street food on offer in Khayelitsha. *Below right:* Examining a diamond at Prins and Prins, creators of exquisite custom-made diamond jewellery. *Above:* The casual bustle of the Oranjezicht City Farm Market at the historic Granger Bay site in the V&A Waterfront. Here independent local farmers and artisanal food producers offer their wares and inspire a new, fresh approach to organic food and cooking.

Labotessa ::: Labotessa

Das stylishe Labotessa Luxury Boutique Hotel gehört zu den vielen architektonischen Perlen rund um Kapstadts Church Square, benannt nach der Groote Kerk (Afrikaans: Große Kirche) aus dem 19. Jahrhundert, deren Geschichte als ältestes christliches Gotteshaus in Südafrika bis 1678 zurückreicht. Eine Tafel in der Nähe erinnert an den Sklavenhandel, der früher auf dem Platz stattfand, ein Hinweis auf einen Aspekt des einstigen Lebens am Kap. ::: The stylish Labotessa Luxury Boutique Hotel nestles among the many architectural gems that line Cape Town's landmark Church Square, named after the Groote Kerk ("Great Church") built in the mid-1800s. Its heritage, however, dates back to 1678 and is the oldest site of Christian worship in South Africa. A nearby plaque commemorates the slave trade that once took place on the square, a reminder of an aspect of early Cape life.

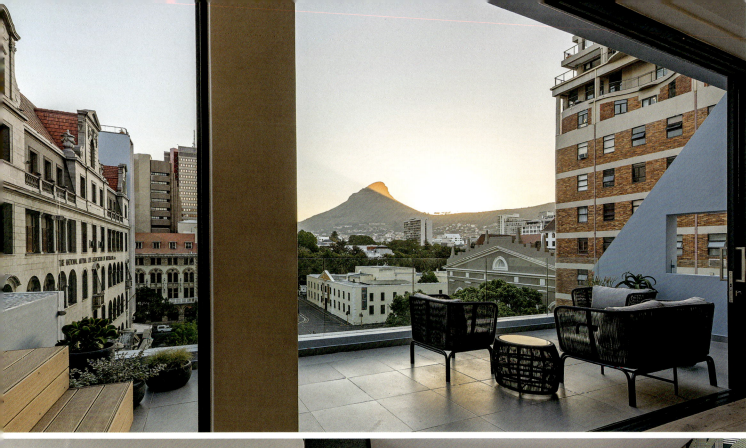

In allen Punkten besticht Labotessa durch zurückhaltende Eleganz und Raffinesse – liebevoll gepflegte historische Elemente verschmelzen bruchlos mit dem feinen zeitgenössischen Design der Suiten und Empfangsräume. ::: Understated elegance and sophistication mark all aspects of Labotessa. Meticulously maintained detail reminiscent of bygone times melds seamlessly with the stylish contemporary design of its reception rooms and suites.

Stille Opulenz erfüllt alle Suiten des Hotels, aber die Präsidenten-Suite erhebt sie zu einer wahren Oase von Frieden und Luxus im Herzen dieser pulsierenden Stadt. Der Blick von Pool und Balkon reicht bis zum Lion's Head, dem westlichen Begleiter des Tafelbergs, und hinunter auf den Platz und zur Slave Lodge, wo regelmäßig Ausstellungen Aufmerksamkeit auf die Menschenrechte lenken. ::: Quiet opulence suffuses all the hotel's suites, but the Presidential Suite is a step up, an oasis of peace and luxury in Cape Town's vibrant heart. The view from the pool and balcony extends towards Lion's Head, Table Mountain's western cohort, and down into the square and the Slave Lodge, where a regular flow of temporary exhibitions highlights human rights awareness.

Im Erdgeschoss steht Labotessa's Café & Terrace den Hotelgästen und der Allgemeinheit offen. Hier kann man sich treffen, bei Bier und Wein entspannen oder sogar Kräuter-Gin-Tonic aus der Region probieren. ::: Situated on the ground floor and open to guests and to the public, Labotessa's Café & Terrace is a place to meet and relax over a beer, wine or even a locally made botanically-infused Gin & Tonic.

Café und Terrasse gehen auf das Kopfsteinpflaster des Church Square hinaus, der als nationales Kulturdenkmal erst vor Kurzem einer unrühmlichen Existenz als Parkplatz entronnen ist. Das beliebte Lokal ist berühmt für sein Ganztags-Frühstück und die Biogerichte aus fairem, nachhaltigem Anbau. ::: The Café flows out onto the Terrace and beyond onto the cobbled Church Square, a national heritage site recently reclaimed from an inglorious carpark. The popular eatery is renowned for its all-day breakfast selection, and a menu founded on ethically-sourced, organic produce.

Bildende Kunst & Street-Art ::: Fine Art & Street Art

Links: Conrad Hicks, Schmied, Künstler und Werkzeugmacher in seiner Schmiede in The Bijou, einem umgewidmeten Art-déco-Kino in Observatory, Kapstadts originellstem Bohème-Vorort. *Oben:* Kapstadts Straßenkunst-Szene entstand in den 1980er-Jahren, als Künstler mit Graffiti ihrer Wut über das Apartheidsystem Luft machten. Heute gehört Street-Art ganz respektabel zu Kapstadts Wahrzeichen – der schwimmende Elefant stammt von Falko One, einem der einflussreichsten Graffitikünstler Südafrikas.
::: *Left:* Conrad Hicks, blacksmith, toolmaker and artist, at work in his forge in The Bijou, a repurposed art deco cinema in Cape Town's quirky, most bohemian suburb of Observatory. *Above:* Cape Town's street art tradition emerged in the 1980s when graffiti gave artists a platform to express their anger towards the apartheid system. Today, street art is a mainstream feature of Cape Town – this swimming elephant is the work of Falko One, one of South Africa's most influential graffiti artists.

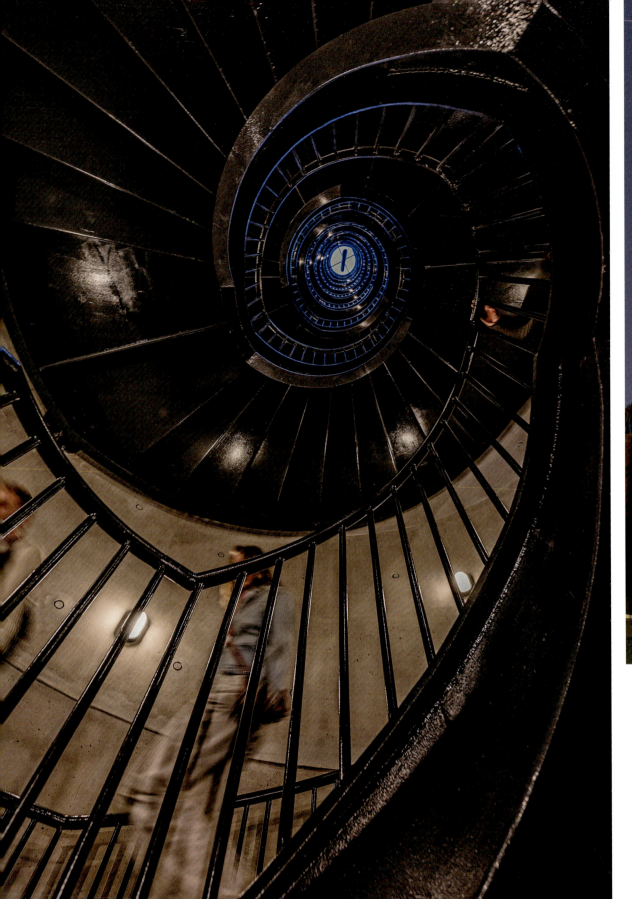

Innen- und Außenansicht des Zeitz Museum of Contemporary Art Africa. Das öffentliche nicht kommerzielle und zeitgenössische Museum sammelt Kunst des 21. Jahrhunderts aus Afrika und dessen Diaspora, bewahrt, forscht und stellt sie aus. ::: Interior and exterior of the Zeitz Museum of Contemporary Art Africa, a public, not-for-profit contemporary art museum that collects, preserves, researches and exhibits 21st-century art from Africa and its diaspora.

Street-Art auf einer baufälligen Wand im innerstädtischen Woodstock-Viertel. Bei einem Bummel kann man die lebendige Kunstform kennen- und schätzen lernen. Die meisten der häufig zu Unrecht negativ konnotierten Kunstwerke sind Auftragsarbeiten, immer ausgeführt mit Erlaubnis der Besitzer. Das Anliegen, abgesehen davon, auf soziale oder ökologische Missstände aufmerksam zu machen, ist, in verarmten Bezirken eine anregende, freundlichere Umgebung zu schaffen. ::: Street art on a dilapidated wall in the inner-city suburb of Woodstock where a walking tour is the best way to learn about and to appreciate this vibrant art form. Attitudes towards graffiti are often pejorative, but this is misguided as most of the works are commissioned and always done with permission from the building owners. The objective, aside from drawing attention to social and environmental injustice, is to create engaging, more pleasant surroundings in impoverished areas.

Entspannung & Sport ::: **Relaxation & Sport**

Gegenüberliegende Seite: Gedränge in Camps Bay, einem von zehn Stränden im Stadtgebiet, die den Blue-Flag (Blaue Flagge)-Status genießen. Dieses internationale Gütezeichen wird an Strände verliehen, die in Umwelterziehung und Information, sowie in Wasserqualität, Sauberkeit, Sicherheit und Service hervorragend sind. *Oben:* Start der jährlichen Cape Town Cycle Tour. 35.000 Radrennfahrer aus der ganzen Welt nehmen die 109 Kilometer der wohl schönsten Rennstrecke weltweit in Angriff.

::: *Opposite page:* A crowded Camps Bay beach, one of ten in Cape Town area to have Blue Flag status. This international accreditation is awarded to beaches displaying excellence in environmental education and information, water quality, environmental management, and safety and services. *Above:* The start of the annual Cape Town Cycle Tour which sees 35,000 cyclists from around the world tackle the 109km route, regarded as the most beautiful bike race in the world.

Man trifft sich zum Sundowner an einem langen, sonnendurchtränkten Sommerabend mit Blick auf die lang gestreckte Weite des Noordhoek-Strands. Am südlichen Strandende liegt das Dörfchen Kommetije zwischen den Bergen und der See. ::: Meeting up for sundowners on a long, sun-drenched summer evening, overlooking the long uninterrupted sweep of Noordhoek Beach. At the southern tip of the beach, the village of Kommetjie nestles between the mountains and the sea.

Ganz oben rechts: Wanderung auf dem Bergwegenetz der Kap-Halbinsel.
Oben: Start des jährlichen 240 Kilometer langen Berg-River-Kanu-Marathons.
::: *Top and right:* Hiking along the Peninsula's network of mountain paths.
Above: The start of the 240-kilometre annual Berg River canoe marathon.

Das riesige Mehrzweckstadion am Fuß von Signal Hill wurde für die FIFA-Weltmeisterschaft 2010 gebaut. Heute ist die größte Veranstaltung der Kapstadt-Teil der internationalen Siebener-Rugby-Turniere, bei denen etwa 120.000 Fans für das dreitägige Fest durch die Tore der Arena strömen. ::: The massive multipurpose Cape Town Stadium at the foot of Signal Hill was built for the 2010 FIFA World Cup. The biggest event is now the Cape Town leg of the International Sevens rugby competition when some 120,000 fans stream through the gates over the three-day festival.

Oben: Entspannen auf einem SUP-Board vor Clifton's Forth Beach, im Hintergrund die Zwölf Apostel, die Gipfelkette, die vom Tafelberg aus südwärts läuft. *Rechts:* Kitesurfen ist – wie Stand-Up-Paddeln – ein Newcomer in Kapstadts Wassersporttradition, hat sich aber innerhalb kürzester Zeit zu einem populären Sport entwickelt. Es passt ideal zu Kapstadts oft windigen Bedingungen, besonders entlang der Westküste der Stadt von Milnerton bis hinauf zur Big Bay in Blaauwberg. ::: *Above:* Relaxing on a stand-up paddleboard off Clifton's Forth Beach against the backdrop of the Twelve Apostles, the row of peaks running southwards from Table Mountain. *Right:* Kite surfing, like stand-up paddleboarding, is a relative newcomer to Cape Town's water sports tradition, but it has snowballed in popularity. It is ideally suited to Cape Town's often windy conditions, especially along the city's West Coast from Milnerton through to Big Bay in Blaauwberg.

Babylonstoren ::: **Babylonstoren**

Ein Meer von tieforangen Clivien – nur ein Höhepunkt von vielen in Babylonstorens ausgedehnten Gärten. Die Geschichte des berühmten Guts beginnt mit der niederländischen Besiedlung des Kaps im Jahr 1692. Sein Name leitet sich vom konischen Hügel oberhalb der Farm ab. Das gutseigene Weinmuseum *(oben)* zeigt Südafrikas faszinierende Weinbaugeschichte, während im unterirdischen Keller Tontöpfe aus Italien Gedanken an die Winzertechniken des alten Rom wachrufen. ::: A swathe of deep orange-red clivias, one of the many highlights of Babylonstoren's sprawling gardens. The story of the renowned estate dates back to 1692 and the beginning of the Dutch settlement at the Cape. The intriguing name derives from the conical hill rising above the farm. The estate's wine museum *(top)* explores South Africa's intriguing viticultural history, while, in the subterranean cellar, Italian-made clay pots pay homage to the wine-making techniques of ancient Rome.

Babylonstorens leidenschaftliches Engagement für Handwerkskunst wird spürbar in der einladenden Stille des Scented Room (Engl.: parfümiert). Hier finden sich die frischen, süßen Noten von Rosmarin, Lavendel und anderen Kräutern aus dem Gutsgarten in Seifen, Kerzen und anderen Produkten. Und nahebei wird feinstes Olivenöl hergestellt *(ganz rechts)*. ::: Babylonstoren's passionate, artisanal approach is embodied in the embracing tranquillity of the Scented Room. Here, the fresh, sweet overtones of rosemary, lavender, and other plants harvested from the estate's gardens are used in a range of soaps, candles, and other products. Nearby, fine, virgin olive oils are made *(far right)*.

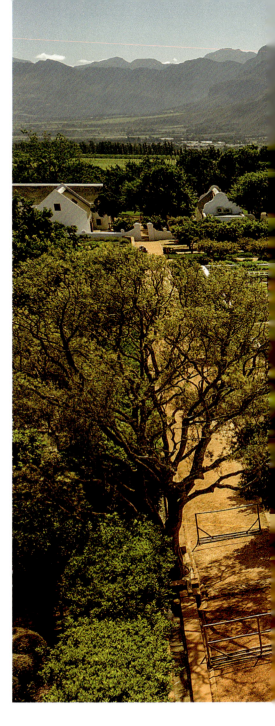

Die Dinge einfach und natürlich zu halten, darin liegt die Essenz von Babylonstoren, von der Winzerei und dem Brotbacken bis zum Züchten von Chianina-Rindern, sicherlich der feinsten Rinderrasse der Welt. Aber das Herz der Farm ist fraglos der geometrisch angelegte Garten, der an die einstige Bedeutung des Kaps als Proviantstation für durchreisende Segelschiffe erinnert. ::: Keeping things simple and true to Nature is the essence of Babylonstoren, from the making of fine wines to bread-making and raising grass-fed Italian Chianina cattle, arguably the finest beef breed in the world. But the heart of the farm is undoubtedly the formal garden redolent of the Cape's importance as a victualing station for passing sailing ships.

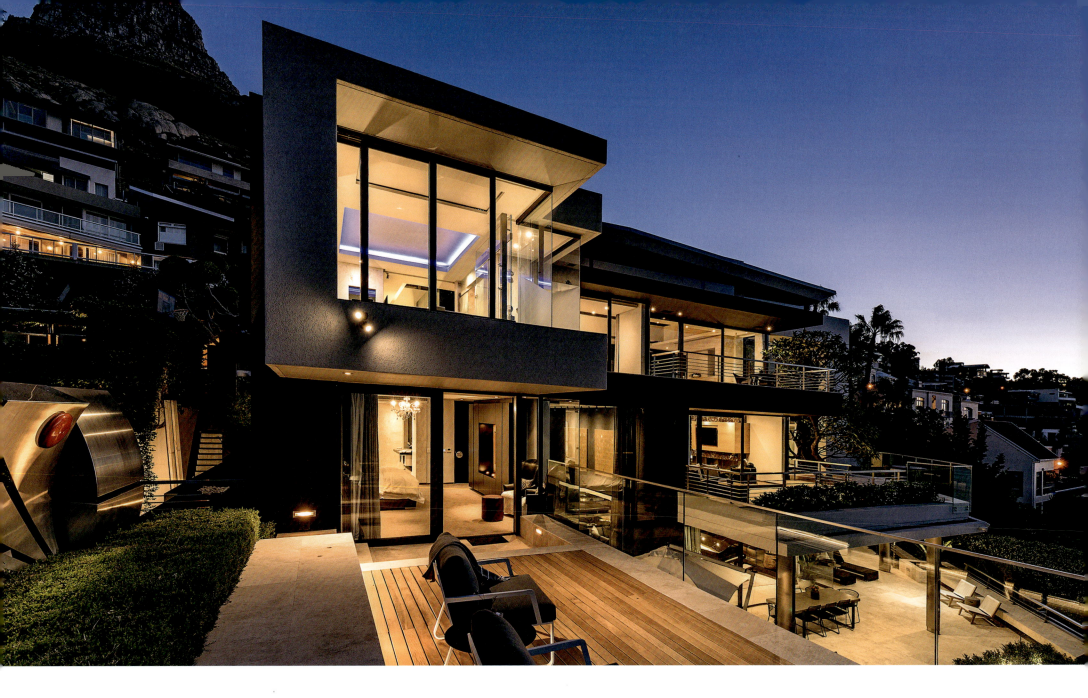

Moderne Architektur & Klassische Bauten
::: Modern Architecture & Vintage Buildings

Gegenüberliegende Seite: Moondance, eine der vielen Villen und Wohnhäuser, die sich an die steilen Hänge von Bantry Bay schmiegen, unterhalb vom Sandsteingipfel des Lion's Head. Vor dem Ersten Weltkrieg hieß der Stadtteil noch Botany Bay, nach längst verschwundenen Gärten, wo man medizinische Kräuter anbaute. Heute stehen in dieser geschützten Bucht einige der begehrtesten Immobilien Kapstadts. *Oben:* Die imposante Jameson Hall gehört zur Universität von Kapstadt.
::: *Opposite page:* Moondance, one of the many villas and apartment blocks that cling to the steep slopes of Bantry Bay beneath the sandstone peak of Lion's Head. Formerly known as Botany Bay after long-gone gardens where medicinal herbs were once cultivated, the suburb's name was changed during World War I. Today, this sheltered cove is the setting of some of Cape Town's most sought-after real estate. *Above:* The imposing edifice of the University of Cape Town's Jameson Hall.

Die Skyline des Küstenvorlands mit dem Cape Town International Conference Centre im Vordergrund. Dieses Gebiet ist der Mittelpunkt von Kapstadts Geschäftsdistrikt und lag bis in die 1940er-Jahre noch unter Wasser. In einem ehrgeizigen Rückgewinnungsprojekt wurden dem Meer am südlichen und südöstlichen Ufer der Tafelbucht wieder 194 Hektar Land abgetrotzt. ::: The city's foreshore skyline with the Cape Town International Conference Centre in the foreground. Today the area is the focus of Cape Town's CBD, but until the 1940s it was underwater. In an ambitious reclamation project, 194 hectares were won back from the sea along the southern and south-eastern shores of Table Bay.

Der Weinkeller in riesenhafter Korkenzieherform steht im Ellerman-House-Hotel in Bantry Bay. Diese elegante Villa im edwardianischen Kap-Stil entstand 1906. Nach einer ausgedehnten Restaurierungs- und Renovierungsphase ab 1988 wurde das markante Gebäude 1992 als ein kleines, exklusives Hotel wiedereröffnet. ::: The giant corkscrew design of the wine cellar at the Ellerman House hotel and villa complex in Bantry Bay. This elegant Cape Edwardian mansion dates back to 1906, but after an extensive restoration and renovation project started in 1988, the landmark mansion opened as a small, exclusive hotel in 1992.

Architektonische Details von drei Kultorten. *Ganz oben:* Die Decke der griechisch-orthodoxen Kathedrale in Woodstock. *Oben:* Die Orgel der Niederländisch-reformierten Kirche in der Buitenkant Street. *Rechts:* Die Freimaurerloge in der Parliament Street. ::: Architectural details from three iconic city buildings. *Top:* The ceiling of the Greek Orthodox Cathedral in Woodstock. *Above:* The organ pipes of the Nederduitse Gereformeerde Kerk in Buitenkant Street. *Right:* The Masonic Lodge in Parliament Street.

Eine Fußgängerbrücke auf Stelzen im Cape Town International Conference Centre, das die City in das wichtigste Ziel für Geschäftstourismus in Afrika verwandelt hat. ::: The elevated walkway linking the exhibition facilities of the Cape Town International Conference Centre which has made the city the prime business tourism destination in Africa.

Die verschlungenen Fenster der Suiten im nahe gelegenen Silo-Hotel erlauben Panoramablicke über den Hafen hinweg auf das ferne Ufer der Tafelbucht und die Westküsten-Vororte Milnerton und Blaauwberg. ::: The intricate window design of the suites in the nearby Silo hotel, provide panoramic views across the harbour to the far shore of Table Bay and the West Coast suburbs of Milnerton and Blaauwberg.

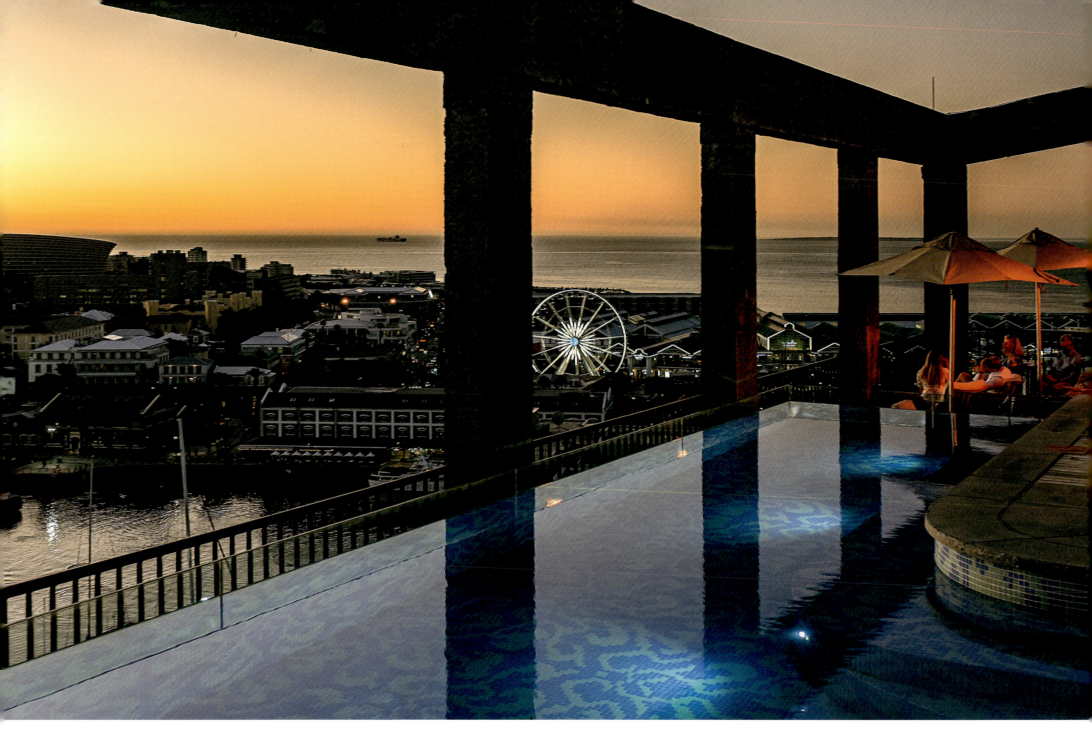

Die Poolterrasse des Royal Portfolio Silo Hotels an der V&A Waterfront. ::: The pool deck of the Royal Portfolio's Silo Hotel in the V&A Waterfront.

Edwardianische Pracht der Cape Town City Hall, wo das Cape Town Philharmonic Orchestra zu Hause ist.
::: Edwardian grandeur of Cape Town City Hall, home of the Cape Town Philharmonic Orchestra.

Moderner Luxus – ein Privathaus an den Hängen des Helderbergs in der rasant wachsenden Stadt Somerset West, circa 45 Kilometer östlich von Kapstadt. :::
Modern luxury – a private home perched on the slopes of the Helderberg in the rapidly growing town of Somerset West, some 45 kilometres east of Cape Town.

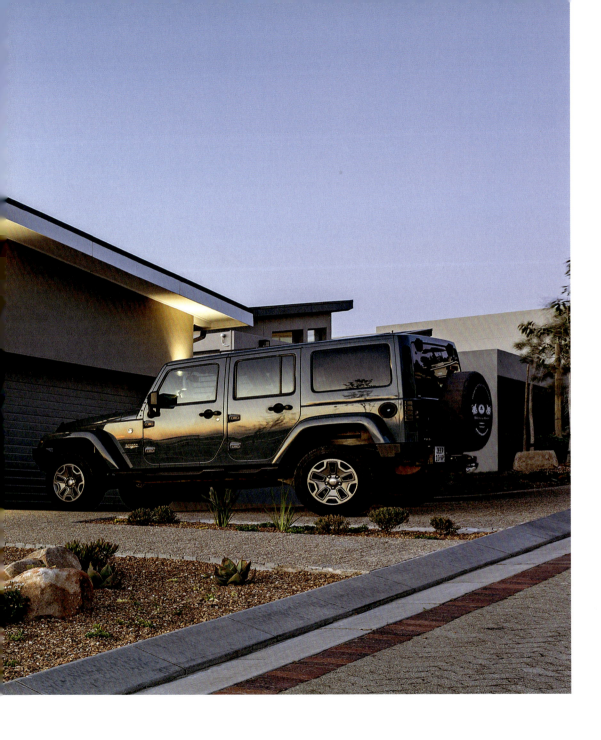

Rosen und Meer – die schwarz-weiß gekachelte Veranda eines viktorianischen Hauses an Kapstadts Atlantikküste.
::: Roses and sea – the black-and-white tiled veranda of a Victorian-period home on Cape Town's Atlantic seaboard.

Links unten: Der wohl weltweit einzige Designer-Dachgarten mit Airstream-Wohnwagenpark gehört zum Grand Daddy Boutique Hotel auf Kapstadts Long Street Strip. Er ist sicher eine der flippigsten Übernachtungsmöglichkeiten der Stadt. *Rechts unten:* Das gesetztere Art-déco-Ambiente im Old-Mutual-Gebäude. Der frühere Hauptsitz einer Versicherung ist inzwischen zu Luxusapartments umgebaut worden. ::: *Left below:* Billed as the only designer rooftop Airstream trailer park in the world, the Grand Daddy Boutique Hotel on the city's Long Street Strip is certainly one of the funkiest places to stay in Cape Town. *Right below:* The more sedate art deco interior of the city's Old Mutual Building, once the headquarters of an insurance company and now repurposed as a luxury apartment block.

Knallig bunte Häuser in Bo-Kaap, buchstäblich „Über dem Kap", einer kleinen, überwiegend muslimischen Enklave über der City am Hang des Signal Hill. Bo-Kaap ist das älteste noch existierende Wohnviertel Kapstadts, und seine Geschichte geht bis in die 1760er-Jahre zurück. 19 Orte des Stadtteils sind nationale Kulturerbestätten, und es gibt die größte Architekturdichte von Gebäuden vor 1850 in Südafrika. ::: Brightly coloured homes of the Bo-Kaap, literally "Above Cape", a small predominantly Muslim enclave above the city on the slopes of Signal Hill. The suburb is the oldest surviving residential neighbourhood in the city, dating back to the 1760s. Some 19 sites in the Bo-Kaap have been declared national heritage monuments and the suburb has the largest concentration of pre-1850 architecture in South Africa.

Quoin Rock ::: Quoin Rock

Das Weingut Quoin Rock liegt hoch oben im Knorhoek Valley, direkt vor den imposanten Steilwänden des Simonsbergs. Im Westen, wo der Tafelberg in der Ferne aufragt, liegt der geometrisch-verspielte Manor House Garden, designed von Franchesca Watson, der in einer Reihe von Bäumen oder von Hecken gesäumten „Zimmern" jeweils einen anderen Charakter enthüllt. Die Passion der Besitzer für Rosen spiegelt sich in der reichen Fülle ihrer sorgsam gepflegten Beete. ::: The Quoin Rock Wine Estate nestles into the landscape high in the Knorhoek Valley, with the imposing cliffs of the Simonsberg rising sheer behind. To the west, with Table Mountain in the far distance, lies the formal, yet playful, Manor House Garden, designed by Franchesca Watson, revealed in a series of tree and hedge-bounded "rooms", each with its own character. The owner's passion for roses manifests in their abundance in neatly tended beds.

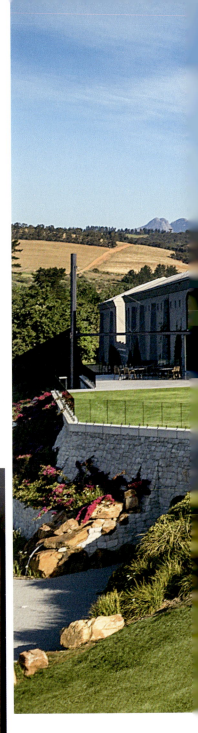

Unter der Leitung von Denis und Yuliya Gaiduk, mit ihrer großen Begeisterung für Kunst und Design, ist der kapholländische Stil des Herrenhauses und seiner Umrahmung geschickt mit der zeitgenössischen Landschaftsgestaltung und der Architektur der Kellerei verschmolzen worden. ::: Under the custodianship of Denis and Yuliya Gaiduk and their deep passion for art and design, the traditional Cape Dutch style of the Manor House and its surrounds have been skillfully melded with the contemporary landscaping and architecture of the estate's winery.

Gåte ist der Ort für ein Gourmet-Erlebnis auf Quoin Rock. Der norwegische Name, ausgesprochen „Go-te", bedeutet „Rätsel" oder „Mysterium" – eine Anspielung auf die kulinarischen Geheimnisse, die die Gäste in diesem raffinierten Restaurant erwarten. ::: Gåte is the venue for a fine dining experience at Quoin Rock. The name, pronounced "gah-tey", suggests a riddle or enigma in Norwegian – an appropriate allusion to the unfolding culinary experience awaiting guests at this sophisticated restaurant.

Die Autoren ::: The Authors

Peter Borchert, Alain Proust, Thomas Ernst

Alain Proust

Der Fotograf wurde in Frankreich geboren und dort ausgebildet. Vor fast 50 Jahren ließ er sich als kommerzieller Fotograf in Kapstadt nieder. Seine vielfältigen Interessen führten zu Arbeiten an verschiedenen Büchern über Essen, Wein, Architektur und Landschaften als wiederkehrende Themen. Seit Jahrzehnten gilt er als einer der besten Fotografen seiner Generation in Südafrika. Mit unverminderter Leidenschaft ist er immer noch sehr aktiv.

The photographer was born and educated in France. He settled in Cape Town almost 50 years ago, working as a commercial photographer. His various interests lead him to work on various books, food, wine, architecture and landscapes being the recurrent themes. For decades he has been regarded as one of the best photographers of his generation in South Africa. He is still very active with his passion never fading.

Thomas Ernst

Bereits seit seiner Jugend interessierte sich Thomas Ernst für Fotografie. Wann auch immer es seine Zeit zuließ, bereiste er viele Länder der Welt sowohl beruflich als auch privat. Er fotografierte und schrieb Berichte für verschiedene Publikationen und gab einige Bücher zu unterschiedlichen Themen auch im Delius Klasing Verlag heraus. Eines seiner Hobbies ist, gutes Essen zu genießen und dazu hervorragende Weine zu entdecken. Nicht zuletzt führten ihn genau diese Interessen nach Südafrika, was mit Abstand zu seinen Lieblingszielen auf der Welt gehört. Das entscheidende Talent des Rheinländers Thomas Ernst ist es, Menschen international miteinander zu vernetzen und für komplexe Projekte zu begeistern. Genau mit dieser Gabe entstand die Idee zu diesem Buch. So gelang es ihm auch hier, den Spitzenfotograf Alain Proust und den namhaften Autor Peter Borchert zur Erstellung des Manuskripts des Buches „Kapstadt – Stadt der Gegensätze" ins Boot zu holen.

Thomas Ernst's interest in photography goes right back to his youth. He travelled, time permitting, to many countries in the world, professionally as well as privately. He took photographs and wrote reports for various publications and edited a number of books on different subjects, among others for the publisher Delius Klasing. One of his hobbies is fine dining in combination with the discovery of excellent wines. These very interests led him not last to South Africa, which is, by far, his worldwide favourite travel destination. Rhinelander Thomas Ernst has one crucial talent, his ease at networking internationally, connecting people and winning their enthusiasm for complex projects. This gift precisely has led to the idea for the present

Danksagung ::: Authors Acknowledgements

book. And he has achieved it again: Top-photographer Alain Proust and renowned author Peter Borchert are on board to create the manuscript for "Cape Town – City full of Contrasts".

Peter Borchert

Peter Borchert ist Autor und Naturschützer und engagiert sich schon ein Leben lang für Afrikas Natur- und Kulturerbe. Er genießt hohes Ansehen für seine kritischen Leitartikel und als ein unabhängiger, ortskundiger Kommentator zu afrikanischen Belangen.

He is a writer, conservationist and lifetime champion of Africa's wild places and cultural heritage. He is highly regarded for his probing editorials and as an independent commentator on and about Africa.

Wir bedanken uns herzlich bei allen Unterstützern, die diese Buchidee möglich gemacht haben. Dazu gehören vor allem die Menschen, die uns Tür und Tor geöffnet haben, um uns ohne Einschränkung mit der Kamera an ihrer Welt teilhaben zu lassen. Sie haben uns an ihre Lieblingsorte in und um Kapstadt, eine der schönsten Städte der Welt, mitgenommen.

Unser Dank gilt ganz besonders auch jenen Weggefährten, die immer an das Buch geglaubt haben. Dazu gehört Dr. Nadja Kneissler von Delius Klasing, die mit ihrer unverwechselbaren Art unser „Motor" für den Start dieser aufwendigen Publikation war. Stephanie Jaeschke, unsere Lektorin, und Jörg Weusthoff, unser Layouter, gehören ebenfalls dazu. Beide haben in beharrlicher Geduld alle unsere Wünsche und häufigen Änderungen in die Tat umgesetzt.

Es war uns allen eine ganz besondere Ehre und ein besonderes Privileg, eine der schönsten Regionen der Welt für dieses Buch bereisen, erleben und darstellen zu dürfen.

We would like to express our warmest thanks to all supporters who have made this book project possible. This goes particularly for all the people who opened their homes and businesses to us, allowing us unreservedly to share their world by camera. They have taken us to their favourite spots in and around Cape Town, one of the world's most beautiful cities.

Our special thanks go also to those traveling companions who have always believed in the book. There is Dr. Nadja Kneissler of Delius Klasing who was, in her own inimitable way, our "motor" for starting this demanding publication. Stephanie Jaeschke, our editor, and Jörg Weusthoff, our art editor, with dogged patience, unstintingly carried through all our wishes and frequent alterations.

It has been a very special honour and a particular privilege to be able to travel, to experience and to portray one of the most beautiful regions of the world for this book.

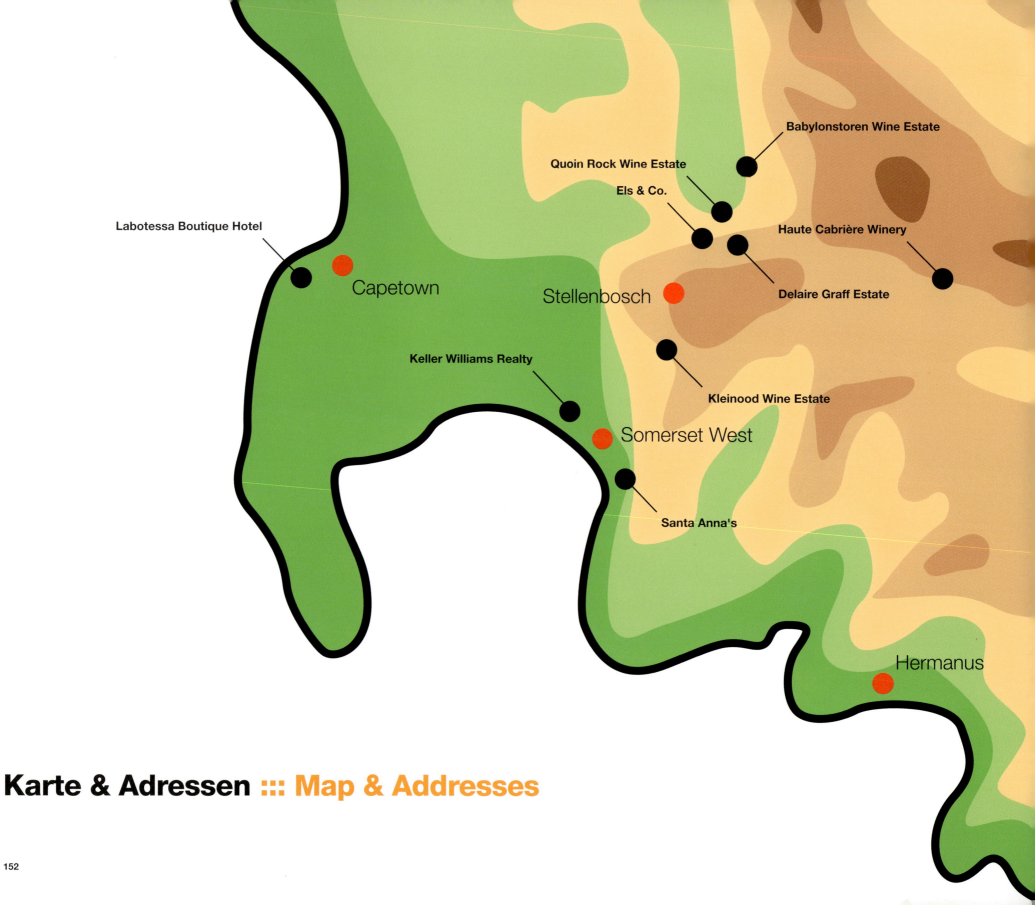

Karte & Adressen ::: **Map & Addresses**

Adressen ::: Addresses

Babylonstoren Wine Estate (S./P. 124)
Klapmuts – Simondium Rd,
Simondium, 7670
+27 21 863 3852
enquiries@babylonstoren.com
www.babylonstoren.com

Delaire Graff Estate (S./P. 48)
Helshoogte Rd,
Stellenbosch, 7602
+27 21 885 8160
info@delaire.co.za
www.delaire.co.za

Els & Co. (S./P. 96)
The Old Dairy,
Rustenberg Wine Farms, Lelie,
Stellenbosch, 7600
+27 21 887 8063
orders@elsfineleather.co.za
www.elsfineleather.com

Haute Cabrière Winery (S./P. 78)
Lambrechts Rd,
Franschhoek, 7690
+27 21 876 8500
info@cabriere.co.za
www.cabriere.co.za

Kleinood Wine Estate (S./P. 62)
Upper Blaauwklippen Rd,
Stellenbosch, 7600
+27 21 880 2527
office@kleinood.com
www.kleinood.com

Labotessa Boutique Hotel (S./P. 106)
5 Church Square,
37 Parliament Street, Cape Town, 8001
+27 21 010 6600
stay@labotessa.com
www.labotessa.com

Quoin Rock Wine Estate (S./P. 144) & Vineyards
Knorhoek Rd,
Stellenbosch, 7600
+27 21 888 4740
info@quoinrock.co.za
www.quoinrock.co.za

Santa Anna's (S./P. 68)
74 Mountainside Blvd,
Mansfield, Cape Town, 7151
+27 21 856 1553
info@santaannas.co.za
www.santaannas.co.za

Geprüfte und empfohlene Adresse
für Immobilieninteressenten:

Klaus Odenberg
Keller Williams Realty
14 De Beers Avenue, Paardevlei,
G04-G08 Bakers Square, M04 Building
Somerset West 7130
+27 71 129 2823
klaus.odenberg@kwsa.co.za
klausodenberg.kwsouthafrica.co.za

Die Weingärten des Vergelegen-Guts über dem schnell wachsenden Vorort Somerset West, zur Rechten die Waterkloof-Kellerei. Dahinter sieht man die Hochhaus-Küstenbebauung von The Strand und links davon das Dorf Gordon's Bay. ::: The vineyards of Vergelegen Estate overlooking the rapidly growing suburbs of Somerset West and the Waterkloof Winery to the right. The high-rise beachfront of The Strand lies beyond and the village of Gordon's Bay to the left.

Bunt angestrichene Fischerboote in Stompneus Bay. Die Gemeinden entlang der Westküste nördlich von Kapstadt lebten bisher traditionell vom Fischfang. Aber Überfischung und Wilderei gefährden jetzt nicht nur die althergebrachte Lebensweise, sondern das marine Ökosystem als Ganzes. ::: Brightly painted fishing dinghies at Stompneus Bay. The communities along the West Coast north of Cape Town have traditionally relied on fishing as a source of food and income. But overfishing and poaching have endangered this way of life as well as the marine ecosystem as a whole.

Ein flammender Sonnenuntergang in Churchhaven spiegelt sich im stillen Wasser der Langebaan-Lagune nördlich von Kapstadt. :::
A fiery sunset at Churchhaven is mirrored in the still waters of Langebaan Lagoon, north of Cape Town.

Bibliografische Information der Deutschen Nationalbibliothek
Die Deutsche Nationalbibliothek verzeichnet diese Publikation
in der Deutschen Nationalbibliografie; detaillierte bibliografische
Daten sind im Internet über http://dnb.dnb.de abrufbar.

1. Auflage
ISBN 978-3-667-11975-9
© Delius Klasing & Co. KG, Bielefeld

Herausgeber/Publisher: Thomas Ernst
Fotos/Photos: Alain Proust, mit Ausnahme von S. 144, 145, 146 (l. o.), 147, 148 (Mitte): Lionel Henshaw
S. 68 (l. o., l. u., u. M., r. u.), 69: Joe Dreyer, except for P. 144, 145, 146 (t. l.), 147, 148 (center): Lionel Henshaw
S. 68 (t. l., b. l., b. c., b. r.), 69: Joe Dreyer
Text/Lyrics: Peter Borchert
Lektorat/Editor: Stephanie Jaeschke, Michaela Franke
Übersetzung/Translator: Trude Stegmann
Layout/Design: Jörg Weusthoff, www.wundrdesign.de
Lithografie/Lithography: Mohn Media, Gütersloh
Druck/Print: Print Consult, München
Printed in Slovakia 2022

Alle Rechte vorbehalten! Ohne ausdrückliche Erlaubnis des Verlages
darf das Werk weder komplett noch teilweise reproduziert, übertragen
oder kopiert werden, wie z. B. manuell oder mithilfe elektronischer und
mechanischer Systeme inklusive Fotokopieren, Bandaufzeichnung und
Datenspeicherung.

Delius Klasing Verlag, Siekerwall 21, D - 33602 Bielefeld
Tel.: 0521/559-0, Fax: 0521/559-115
E-Mail: info@delius-klasing.de
www.delius-klasing.de

Wie ein gekrümmter Hexenfinger scheint der Felsenkamm der Kap-Halbinsel anklagend nach Süden zu zeigen, hinweg über 6.000 Kilometer ozeanische Wildnis direkt auf die Antarktis. ::: Like the gnarled finger of a witch, the rocky spine of the Cape Peninsula seems to jab accusingly southwards across 6,000 kilometres of ocean wilderness towards Antarctica.